Places we will go:
France
Italy
China
Egypt

PEOPLE OF THE STONE AGE

In the Stone Age, people made tools from stone. They hunted animals and picked plants and berries. They worked out how to make fire.

Stone Age tools

Stone Age people preparing food

TIME TO TIME TRAVEL

Helen Chapman

Contents

MEET THE TIME TRAVEL TWINS

Hi! We're David and Sara, the Time Travel Twins. We have a time machine. It lets us go back in time to **ancient** places. So let's go!

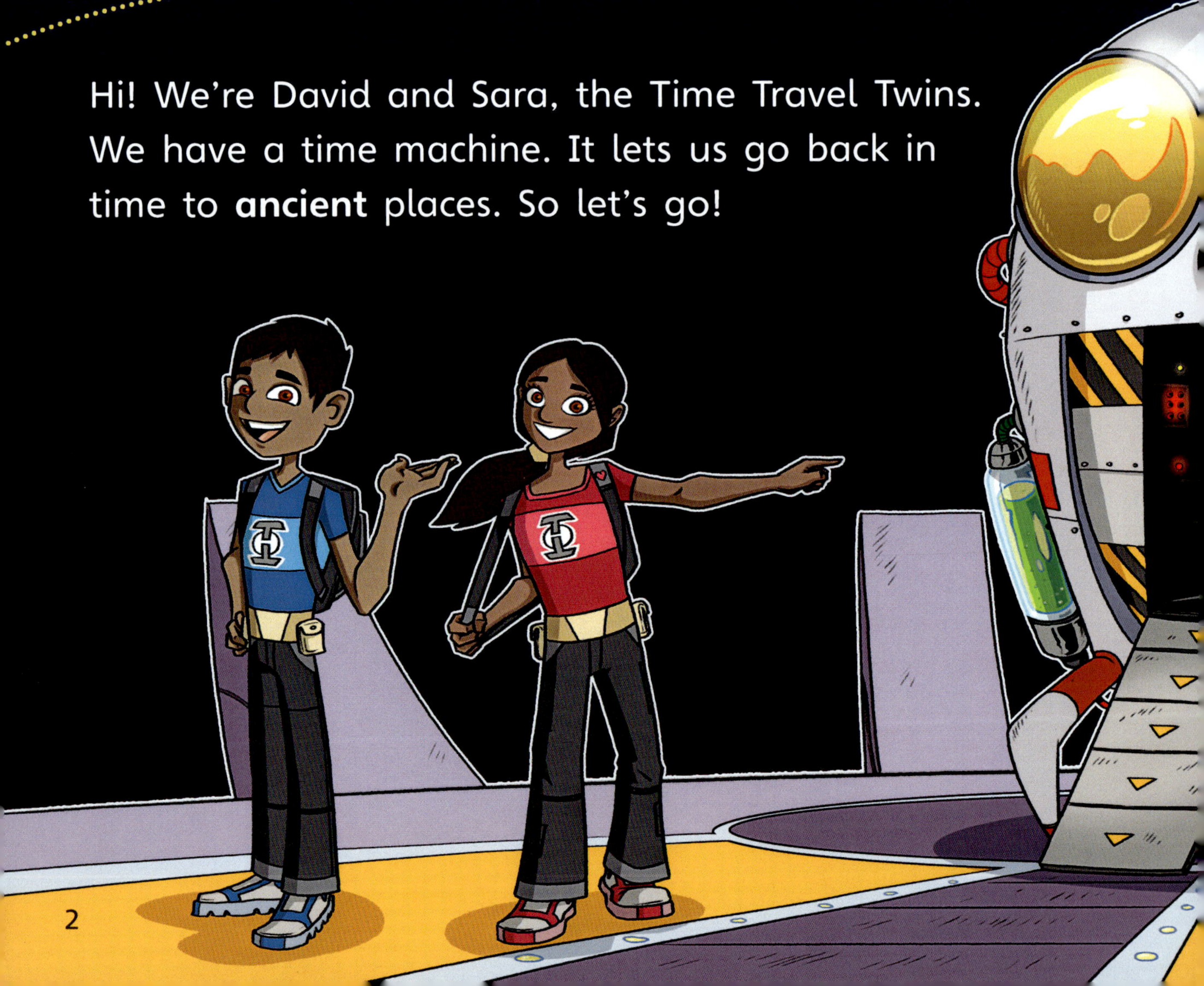

The people of the Stone Age lived in caves. They did paintings about their lives in the caves.

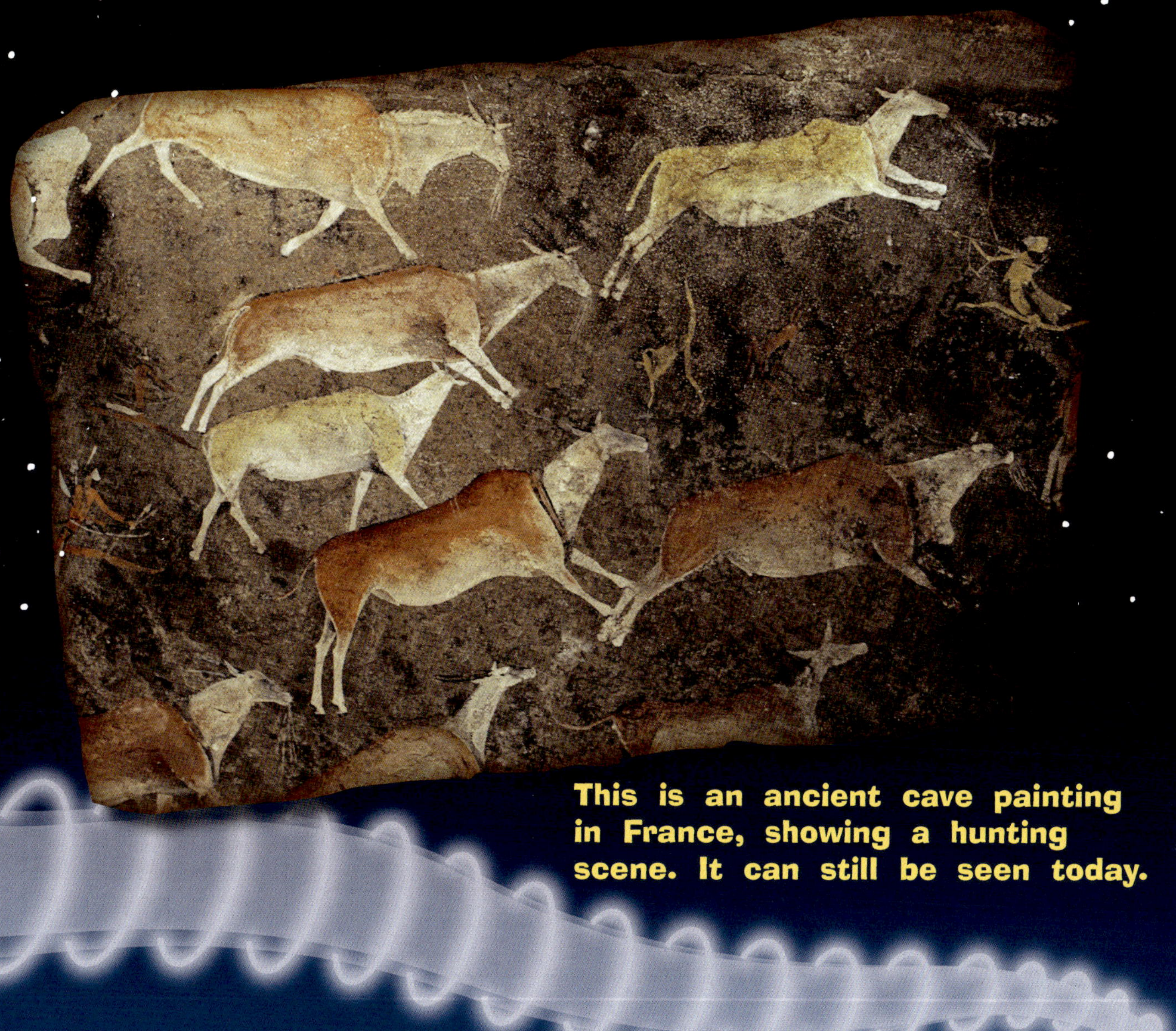

This is an ancient cave painting in France, showing a hunting scene. It can still be seen today.

The people of the Stone Age did not wear clothes. But when it was cold, they would wear animal fur.

STONE AGE PEOPLE:

David: Stone Age people hunted animals such as mammoths, boars and fish.

Sara: And they **invented** tools.

David: Yes! They made tools from stone and wood, such as spears. Smart, hey?

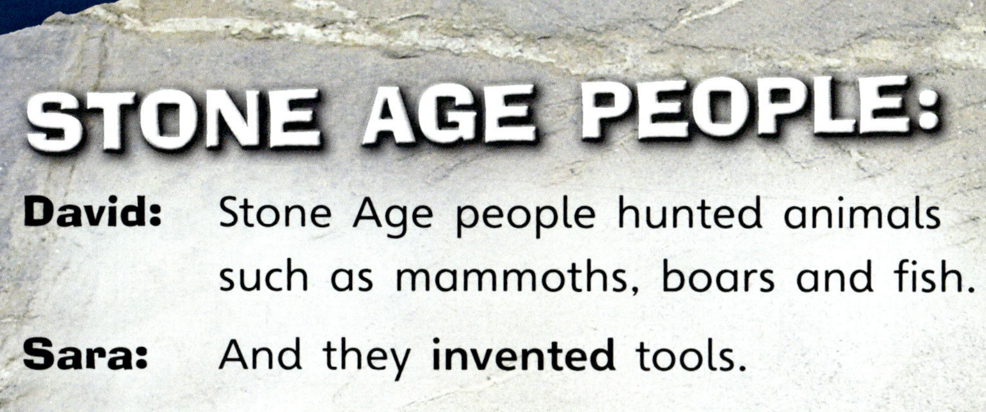

Now let's meet some more clever ancient people – the Egyptians.

THE EGYPTIANS

We've come to Egypt to see amazing Egyptian writing and some famous buildings.

Ancient Egyptian writing was a bit like picture writing. Each sign was a picture of a real thing, like a bird or an eye.

Egyptian writing is called hieroglyphics (say *hi-ra-gli-fiks*).

The Egyptians also built huge **pyramids** and **statues**. The famous statue below has the body of a lion and the head of a king.

It took over 80 years to build the pyramids!

This statue is called the Great Sphinx.

Some ancient Egyptian kings and queens are well-known today.

King Tutankhamen's mummy

King Tutankhamen

Queen Cleopatra

THE KING OF EGYPT
David: I'm nine and I'm King Tutankhamen of Egypt. How cool is that?
Sara: But you die nine years later. You are turned into a **mummy**.
David: But I'll still be a famous king!
Time to go to the other side of the world – China!

LET'S MEET THE CHINESE

The ancient Chinese invented many great things.
They invented:

- paper
- the **compass**
- fireworks.

fireworks

a very old Chinese compass

a Chinese paper scroll

The Chinese had an amazing-looking alphabet, too. They invented a printing press and made books!

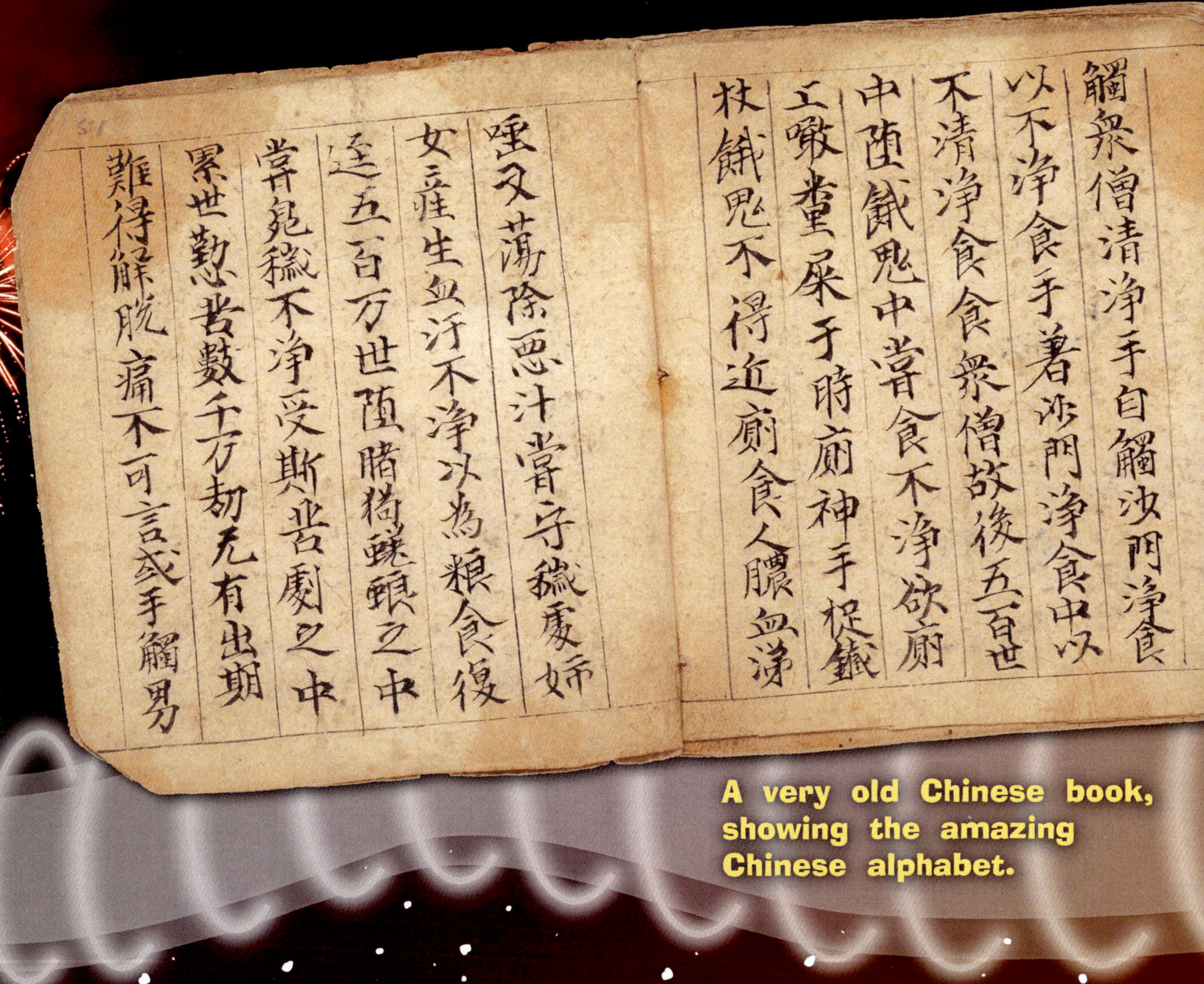

觸衆僧清淨手白觸沙門淨食
以不淨食手著沙門淨食中以
不清淨食衆僧故後五百世
中墮餓鬼中常食不淨欲廁
工噉糞屎手時廁神手捉鐵
杖餓鬼不得近廁食人膿血涕
唾又蕩除惡汁常守獄處婦
女産生血汙不淨以爲粮食復
逕五百万世墮豬狗之中
常飽獄不淨受斯苦處之中
累世歎苦數千万劫无有出期
難得解脫痛不可言或手觸男

A very old Chinese book, showing the amazing Chinese alphabet.

The ancient Chinese built a very famous wall. They built the wall to keep China safe from other countries. It is called the Great Wall of China.

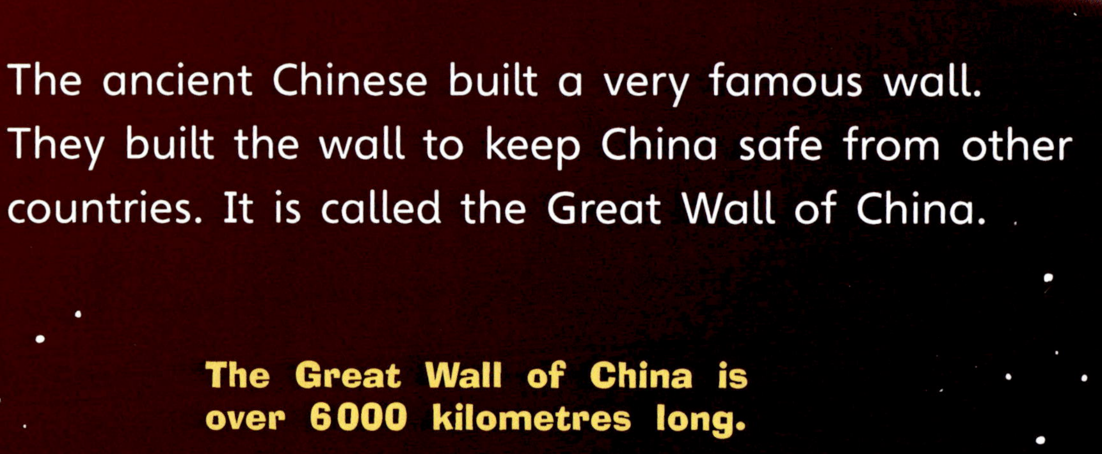

The Great Wall of China is over 6000 kilometres long.

THE GREAT WALL OF CHINA

David: Get some stones and wood, get started!

Sara: Why?

David: We've got to keep China safe.

Sara: But it took 1700 years to make the wall.

David: I didn't say it would be quick!

Time to go! Next stop, Europe!

THE AMAZING ROMANS

The Romans had a huge **Empire**. The Roman army was very strong. They went to war to win other lands.

A ROMAN GLADIATOR

David: I'm a **gladiator**! I'm strong!

Sara: Who cares! Some gladiators had to fight to the death.

David: They did? I'm out of here!

The Romans built many straight roads to link all of their Empire. They also built many amazing buildings.

This is what the Colosseum looks like today. Gladiator fights were held here.

THE CITY OF ROME

Sara: All ancient Roman roads led to Rome.

David: That's why people say "all roads lead to Rome".

GOING BACK AGAIN!

David: That's the end of our trip back in time. We learned about some excellent ancient people.

Sara: I wonder what the ancient people would think if they came to *our* world today?

David: Hmmm... Let's go back in time again and bring them back!

We learned a lot about ancient places. How much can you remember?

1. What place did all roads lead to?
2. Why was the Great Wall of China built?
3. What does the Sphinx look like?
4. What did the Stone Age people eat?

Answers

1. Rome
2. To keep China safe
3. The body of a lion and the head of an Egyptian king
4. Animals, plants and berries

AN ANCIENT TIMELINE

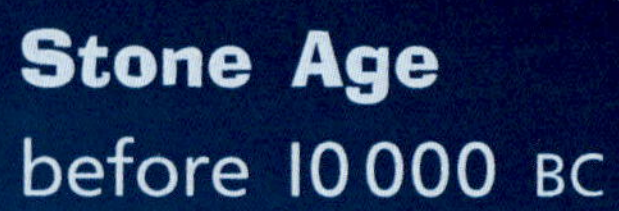

Stone Age
before 10 000 BC

10 000 BC

5 000 BC

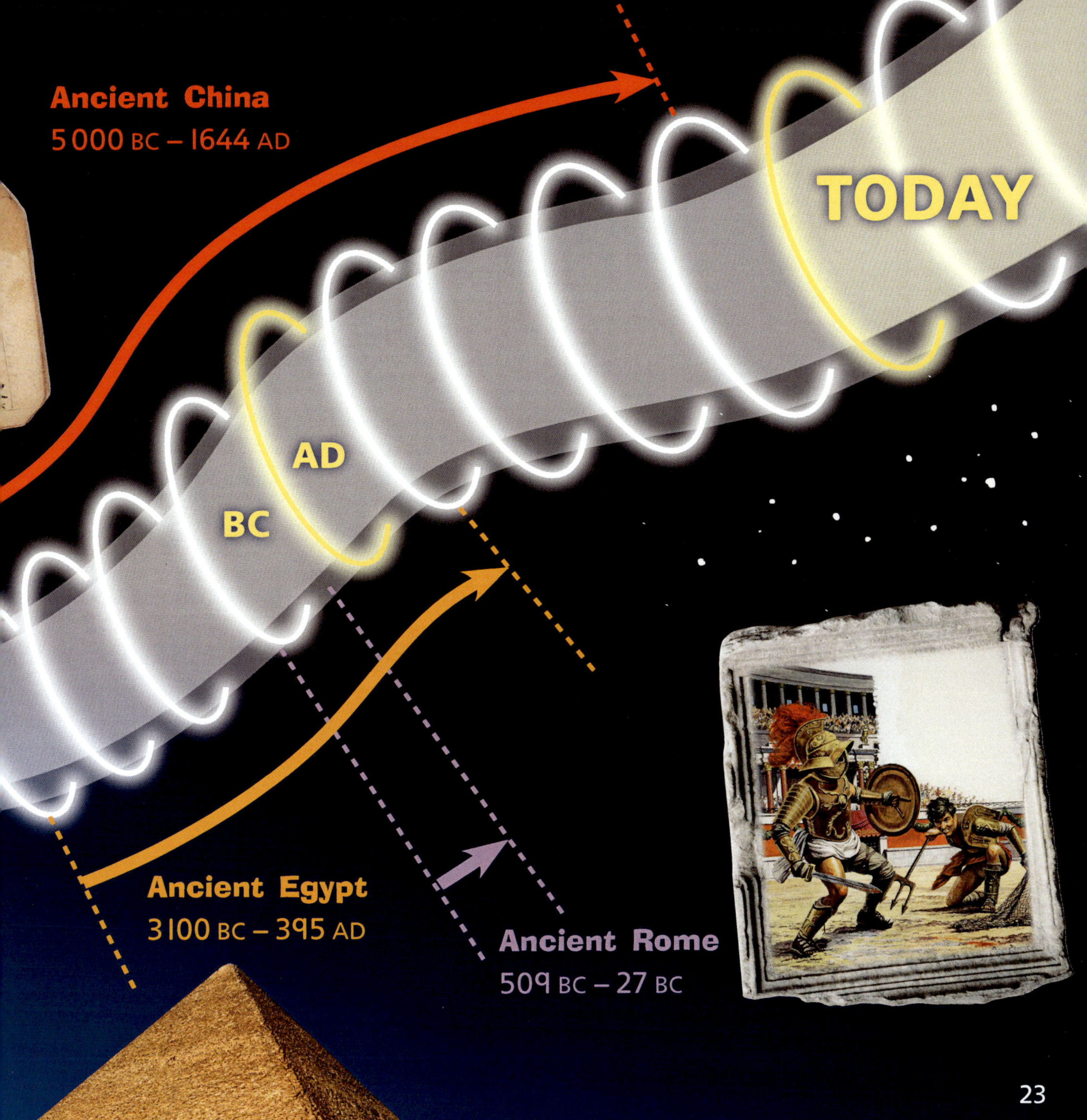
Ancient China
5 000 BC – 1644 AD
TODAY
AD
BC
Ancient Egypt
3100 BC – 395 AD
Ancient Rome
509 BC – 27 BC

GLOSSARY

ancient	very, very old
compass	a tool showing directions such as north, south, east and west
Empire	an area or country ruled by a single Emperor
invented	came up with an idea
gladiator	a slave or professional fighter who entertained the public by fighting to the death
mummy	a dead body that has been made ready for burial
pyramids	tombs for dead Egyptian kings and queens
statues	models of a person or animal made from wood, stone or metal